To

_____

From

_____

365 DAY BRIGHTENERS

BRIGHTENERS

FOR A
Woman's Heart

365 Day Brighteners™ for a Woman's Heart

© 2003 DaySpring Cards, Inc.
Published by Garborg's®, a brand of DaySpring Cards, Inc.
Siloam Springs, Arkansas

Scripture quotations are from the following sources:
The HOLY BIBLE, NEW INTERNATIONAL VERSION®
(NIV)® © 1973, 1978, 1984 by International Bible Society.
Used by permission of Zondervan Publishing House.
THE MESSAGE © Eugene H. Peterson 1993, 1994, 1995.
Used by permission of NavPress Publishing Group. All right
reserved. The Living Bible (TLB) © 1971 by permission of
Tyndale House Publishers, Inc., Wheaton, IL.

Except for Scripture verses, references to men and
masculine pronouns have been replaced with "people,"
"women," and gender-neutral or feminine pronoun.

ISBN 1-58061-738-7   Printed in China

365 DAY BRIGHTENERS

BRIGHTENERS

FOR A Woman's *Heart*

GARBORG'S®

because every day is a gift

T. Williams
2004

*W*hether we are poets or
parents or teachers or artists or gardeners,
we must start where we are and use
what we have. In the process of creation
and relationship, what seems mundane and
trivial may show itself to be holy,
precious, part of a pattern.

LUCI SHAW

JANUARY 1

JANUARY 2

*H*ow wonderful it is
that nobody need wait a single
moment before starting to
improve the world.

ANNE FRANK

*W*e can do no great things,
only small things with great love.

MOTHER TERESA

JANUARY 3

JANUARY 4

*I*t is God to whom and with whom
we travel, and while He is the End of our
journey, He is also at every stopping place.

ELISABETH ELLIOT

*K*nowing what is right is like deep water in the heart; a wise person draws from the well within.

PROVERBS 20:5 THE MESSAGE

JANUARY 5

JANUARY 6

*N*o pessimist ever discovered
the secrets of the stars, or sailed to an
uncharted land, or opened a new heaven
to the human spirit.

HELEN KELLER

A smile is the lighting
system of the face and the heating
system of the heart.

BARBARA JOHNSON

JANUARY 7

JANUARY 8

*J*ust don't give up trying
to do what you really want to do.
Where there is love and inspiration,
I don't think you can go wrong.

ELLA FITZGERALD

*E*ach one of us is God's special work of art. Through us, He teaches and inspires, delights and encourages, informs and uplifts all those who view our lives.

JONI EARECKSON TADA

JANUARY 9

JANUARY 10

*T*he Lord your God...will take great
delight in you, he will quiet you with his
love, he will rejoice over you with singing.

ZEPHANIAH 3:17 NIV

*T*here's something much more important
than taking time and effort to make our
outer being as lovely as possible. We can
tighten our stomach muscles and suck it up,
pay a plastic surgeon to tuck it up, or spend
a lot of money trying to dress it up, but
unless we are growing beautiful on the
inside, our efforts to be glamorous on the
outside are useless.

KATHY PEEL

JANUARY 11

JANUARY 12

*I*f we just give God the little

that we have, we can trust Him to

make it go around.

GLORIA GAITHER

*L*ove is a great beautifier.

LOUISA MAY ALCOTT

JANUARY 13

JANUARY 14

To love what you do and
feel that it matters—how could
anything be more fun?

KATHARINE GRAHAM

$\mathcal{B}$e content with who you are,
and don't put on airs. God's strong
hand is on you; he'll promote you at the
right time. Live carefree before God;
he is most careful with you.

1 PETER 5:6-7 THE MESSAGE

JANUARY 15

JANUARY 16

*W*hen we do what is
right, we have contentment,
peace, and happiness.

BEVERLY LaHAYE

$\mathcal{O}$ur feelings do not affect God's facts. They may blow up, like clouds, and cover the eternal things that we do most truly believe. We may not see the shining of the promises—but they still shine! [His strength] is not for one moment less because of our human weakness.

AMY CARMICHAEL

JANUARY 17

JANUARY 18

*W*here the soul is full of
peace and joy, outward surroundings
and circumstances are of
comparatively little account.

HANNAH WHITALL SMITH

*W*hen we are away from God,
He misses us far more than we miss Him.

RUTH BELL GRAHAM

JANUARY 19

JANUARY 20

*M*ay the God of hope
fill you with all joy and peace
as you trust in him, so that
you may overflow with hope.

ROMANS 15:13 NIV

*A*t the end of your life
you will never regret not having passed
one more test, not winning one more verdict,
or not closing one more deal. You will regret
time not spent with a husband, a friend,
a child, or a parent.

BARBARA BUSH

JANUARY 21

JANUARY 22

*M*any women...have buoyed
me up in times of weariness and stress.
Each friend was important.... Their words
have seasoned my life. Influence, just like
salt shaken out, is hard to see, but
its flavor is hard to miss.

PAM FARREL

*H*aving someone who
understands is a great blessing
for ourselves. Being someone who
understands is a great blessing to others.

JANETTE OKE

JANUARY 23

JANUARY 24

*L*ife varies its stories.
Time changes everything, yet what is
truly valuable—what is worth keeping—
is beyond time.

RUTH SENTER

*C*ome to me and I will
give you rest—all of you who work so hard
beneath a heavy yoke. Wear my yoke—for it
fits perfectly—and let me teach you;
for I am gentle and humble, and you shall
find rest for your souls.

MATTHEW 11:28-29 TLB

JANUARY 25

JANUARY 26

*I*n today's world...it is still women's
business to make life better,
to make tomorrow better than today.

HELEN THAMES RALEY

One can never consent
to creep when one feels
an impulse to soar.

HELEN KELLER

JANUARY 27

JANUARY 28

*T*he secret of joy in work
is contained in one word—excellence.
To know how to do something
well is to enjoy it.

PEARL S. BUCK

*W*e cannot rebuild the world
by ourselves, but we can have a small part
in it by beginning where we are.
It may only be taking care of a neighbor's
child or inviting someone to dinner,
but it is important.

DONNA L. GLAZIER

JANUARY 29

JANUARY 30

*N*othing is impossible with God.

LUKE 1:37 NIV

*N*o tool, in and of itself, has great importance. But placed in the proper hands it can create a masterpiece.

JONI EARECKSON TADA

JANUARY 31

FEBRUARY 1

*H*ere's the test of the
reality of your faith: on whom
does your life depend?

ELISABETH ELLIOT

*W*omen don't want a divided life....
They recognize that career is not enough;
they want to be interconnected with people.
They want to keep growing throughout
their lives, adjusting as needed
to different circumstances.
They want to live a balanced life.

MARY ELLEN ASHCROFT

FEBRUARY 2

FEBRUARY 3

"*H*ope" is the thing with feathers—
That perches in the soul—
And sings the tune without the words—
And never stops—at all.

EMILY DICKINSON

*T*his is my prayer: that your love will flourish and that you will not only love much but well. Learn to love appropriately. You need to use your head and test your feelings so that your love is sincere and intelligent, not sentimental gush.

PHILIPPIANS 1:9-10 THE MESSAGE

FEBRUARY 4

FEBRUARY 5

*W*hat is important is that one
is capable of love. It is perhaps the only
glimpse we are permitted of eternity.

HELEN HAYES

*L*iving simply means
concentrating on what's important
in light of eternity, and not taking
the rest of life too seriously.

ANNIE CHAPMAN

FEBRUARY 6

FEBRUARY 7

*S*ee! The winter is past;

the rains are over and gone.

Flowers appear on the earth;

the season of singing has come.

SONG OF SONGS 2:11-12 NIV

*W*e are weaving the
future on the loom of today.

GRACE DAWSON

FEBRUARY 8

FEBRUARY 9

*T*his is what I have asked of God for you: that you will be encouraged and knit together by strong ties of love, and that you will have the rich experience of knowing Christ with real certainty and clear understanding. For God's secret plan, now at last made known, is Christ himself.

COLOSSIANS 2:2 TLB

*G*ive! Give the love you have received
to those around you. You must love with
your time, your hands, and your hearts.
You need to share all that you have.

MOTHER TERESA

FEBRUARY 10

FEBRUARY 11

I would sooner live in a
cottage and wonder at everything than
live in a castle and wonder at nothing.

JOAN WINMILL BROWN

*T*ry to see the beauty

"in your own backyard,"

to notice the miracles of everyday life.

GLORIA GAITHER

FEBRUARY 12

FEBRUARY 13

*W*hen we give ourselves something to look forward to, no matter how great or small the event, we are giving ourselves the gift of hope. And where there's hope built into tomorrow, there are all kinds of possibilities for overcoming whatever obstacle we face today.

RUTH SENTER

*W*hen two people love each other,

they don't look at each other,

they look in the same direction.

GINGER ROGERS

FEBRUARY 14

FEBRUARY 15

*P*ursue a righteous life—a life
of wonder, faith, love, steadiness, courtesy.
Run hard and fast in the faith. Seize the
eternal life, the life you were called to.

1 TIMOTHY 6:11-12 THE MESSAGE

*W*hat good is a faith if
you can't live it out?

<small>PAM FARREL</small>

FEBRUARY 16

FEBRUARY 17

*W*e live in the present,
we dream of the future, but we learn
eternal truths from the past.

LUCY MAUD MONTGOMERY

*T*ake a risk. Open up your heart.
Find a real friend and grow together.
Be a real friend and see what happens.

SHEILA WALSH

FEBRUARY 18

FEBRUARY 19

*B*ecause of their agelong
training in human relations—for that is
what feminine intuition really is—women
have a special contribution to make to
any group enterprise.

MARGARET MEAD

*T*wo are better than one,
because they have a good return
for their work: If one falls down,
his friend can help him up.

ECCLESIASTES 4:9-10 NIV

FEBRUARY 20

FEBRUARY 21

*H*appiness is not a station
you arrive at, but a manner of traveling.

MARGARET LEE RUNBECK

*S*catter seeds of kindness
everywhere you go;
Scatter bits of courtesy—
Watch them grow and grow.
Gather buds of friendship;
Keep them till full-blown;
You will find more happiness
than you have ever known.

AMY R. RAABE

FEBRUARY 22

FEBRUARY 23

*I*t is possible to be happy without
having perfect health.... Thank goodness
my happiness doesn't come from my joints,
but from my heart.

BEVERLY LAHAYE

*P*eace is not placidity: peace is
The power to endure the megatron of pain
With joy, the silent thunder of release,
The ordering of Love. Peace is the atom's start,
The primal image: God within the heart.

MADELEINE L'ENGLE

FEBRUARY 24

FEBRUARY 25

There is far more to your inner
life than the food you put in your stomach,
more to your outer appearance than the
clothes you hang on your body. Look at the
ravens, free and unfettered, not tied down to
a job description, carefree in the care of
God. And you count far more.

LUKE 12:22-24 THE MESSAGE

$\mathcal{L}$ove is like a violin.
The music may stop now and then,
but the strings remain forever.

JUNE MASTERS BACHER

FEBRUARY 26

FEBRUARY 27

I am not afraid of storms,
for I am learning how to sail my ship.

LOUISA MAY ALCOTT

Snow is falling outside my study
window....I see nature once more playing
endless variations in design and beauty....In
such simply yet eloquent ways, I am reminded
that God is personal, revealing Himself
continuously in the finite.

JUDITH C. LECHMAN

FEBRUARY 28

FEBRUARY 29

I cannot count the number of times I have been strengthened by another woman's heartfelt hug, appreciative note, surprise gift, or caring questions.... My friends are an oasis to me, encouraging me to go on. They are essential to my well-being.

DEE BRESTIN

I love the Lord because he hears
my prayers and answers them.

PSALM 116:1 TLB

MARCH 1

MARCH 2

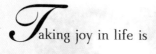aking joy in life is
a woman's best cosmetic.

ROSALIND RUSSELL

*H*ow much of our lives are...
well...so daily. How often our hours are filled
with the mundane, seemingly unimportant
things that have to be done, whether at
home or work. These very "daily" tasks could
become a celebration of praise. "It is through
consecration," someone has said,
"that drudgery is made divine."

GIGI GRAHAM TCHIVIDJIAN

MARCH 3

MARCH 4

*T*think the one lesson I have
learned is that there is no substitute
for paying attention.

DIANE SAWYER

*N*one of us knows what
the next change is going to be, what
unexpected opportunity is just around
the corner, waiting to change all the
tenor of our lives.

KATHLEEN NORRIS

MARCH 5

MARCH 6

*B*ear with each other and
forgive whatever grievances you may have
against one another. Forgive as the
Lord forgave you.

COLOSSIANS 3:13 NIV

*K*eep your face to the sunshine and
you cannot see the shadows.

HELEN KELLER

MARCH 7

MARCH 8

*G*od's friendship is the
unexpected joy we find when
we reach His outstretched hand.

WEAVER SMITH

$\mathcal{W}$hen we live life centered around what others like, feel, and say, we lose touch with our own identity. I am an eternal being, created by God. I am an individual with purpose. It's not what I get from life, but who I am, that makes the difference.

NEVA COYLE

MARCH 9

MARCH 10

*W*hen we put people before
possessions in our hearts, we are sowing
seeds of enduring satisfaction.

BEVERLY LAHAYE

*A*nd God is able to make all grace abound to you, so that in all things at all times, having all that you need, you will abound in every good work.

2 CORINTHIANS 9:8 NIV

MARCH 11

MARCH 12

*N*ot everyone possesses boundless
energy or a conspicuous talent. We are
not equally blessed with great intellect or
physical beauty or emotional strength.
But we have all been given
the same ability to be faithful.

GIGI GRAHAM TCHIVIDJIAN

*G*etting things accomplished
isn't nearly as important as
taking time for love.

JANETTE OKE

MARCH 13

MARCH 14

*C*hoices can change our lives profoundly. The choice to mend a broken relationship, to say "yes" to a difficult assignment, to lay aside some important work to play with a child, to visit some forgotten person—these small choices may affect our lives eternally.

GLORIA GAITHER

*J*oy is warm and radiant
and clamors for expressions
and experience.

DOROTHY SEGOVIA

MARCH 15

MARCH 16

No one lights a lamp, then hides it in a drawer. It's put on a lamp stand so those entering the room have light to see where they're going. Your eye is a lamp, lighting up your whole body. If you live wide-eyed in wonder and belief, your body fills up with light.... Keep your eyes open, your lamp burning, so you don't get musty and murky. Keep your life as well-lighted as your best-lighted room.

LUKE 11:33-36 THE MESSAGE

*Y*ou who have received so much love
show your love by protecting the
sacredness of life.
The sacredness of life is one of the
greatest gifts that God has given us.

MOTHER TERESA

MARCH 17

MARCH 18

I've gone to look for myself.
If I should return before I get back,
keep me here!

BARBARA JOHNSON

*W*hat constitutes success?
She has achieved success who has lived well;
laughed often and loved much; who has
gained the respect of intelligent people and
the love of little children; who has filled her
niche and accomplished her task; who has left
the world better than she found it; who has
always looked for the best in others and
given the best she had.

BESSIE ANDERSON STANLEY

MARCH 19

MARCH 20

*W*hen you are truly joined in spirit,
another woman's good is your good too.
You work for the good of each other.

RUTH SENTER

*I*nstead of looking at the fashions, walk out into the fields and look at the wildflowers. They never primp or shop, but have you ever seen color and design quite like it? The ten best dressed...women in the country look shabby alongside them. If God gives such attention to the appearance of wildflowers...don't you think he'll attend to you, take pride in you, do his best for you?

MATTHEW 6:28-30 THE MESSAGE

MARCH 21

MARCH 22

*F*aith is the first factor in a life devoted to service. Without faith, nothing is possible. With it, nothing is impossible.

MARY MCLEOD BETHUNE

*W*e need time to dream,
time to remember, and time
to reach the infinite. Time to be.

GLADYS TABER

MARCH 23

MARCH 24

*T*o be successful, the first thing
to do is fall in love with your work.

SISTER MARY LAURETTA

*W*e must not, in trying to think about how we can make a big difference, ignore the small daily differences we can make which, over time, add up to big differences that we often cannot foresee.

MARIAN WRIGHT EDELMAN

MARCH 25

MARCH 26

*E*very path he guides us on is
fragrant with his loving-kindness.

PSALM 25:10 TLB

There are approximately 150 billion stars in our galaxy, and scientists believe there are over a billion other galaxies. The God who created all of this is certainly capable of taking care of me!

KATHY PEEL

MARCH 27

MARCH 28

*L*ook at a day when you are
supremely satisfied at the end....
It's when you've had everything to do
and you've done it.

MARGARET THATCHER

I have learned from experience
that the greater part of our happiness
or misery depends on our dispositions
and not on our circumstances.

MARTHA WASHINGTON

MARCH 29

MARCH 30

$\mathcal{T}$he wonder of our Lord is
that He is so accessible to us in the
common things of our lives: the cup
of water...breaking of the bread...welcoming
children into our arms...fellowship over
a meal...giving thanks. A simple attitude
of caring, listening, and lovingly
telling the truth.

NANCIE CARMICHAEL

*W*hy is everyone hungry for more?...

I have God's more-than-enough,

More joy in one ordinary day....

At day's end I'm ready for sound sleep,

For you, God, have put my life back together.

PSALM 4:6-8 THE MESSAGE

MARCH 31

APRIL 1

*F*aith has to be exercised
in the midst of ordinary,
down-to-earth living.

ELISABETH ELLIOT

*I*t is easy to love those who are far away. It isn't always easy to love those who are right next to us. It is easier to offer a dish of rice to satisfy the hunger of a poor person, than to fill up the loneliness and suffering of someone lacking love in our own family.

MOTHER TERESA

APRIL 2

APRIL 3

*L*ove is the seed of all hope.
It is the enticement to trust,
to risk, to try, to go on.

GLORIA GAITHER

*I*ntegrity is a commitment to live
consistently with what you know
to be true about life.

PAM FARREL

APRIL 4

APRIL 5

*C*ling to wisdom—she will protect you.
Love her—she will guard you. Getting wisdom
is the most important thing you can do!
And with your wisdom, develop common
sense and good judgment.

PROVERBS 4:6-7 TLB

$\mathcal{F}$riendship redeems.

It pulls broken parts together

and offers healing.

LUCI SHAW

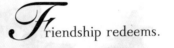

APRIL 6

APRIL 7

*I*t's never too late—in fiction
or in life—to revise.

NANCY THAYER

*B*lue skies with clouds on summer days. A myriad of stars on clear moonlit nights. Tulips and roses and violets and dandelions and daisies. Bluebirds and laughter and sunshine and Easter.

See how He loves us!

ALICE CHAPIN

APRIL 8

APRIL 9

*G*od bless you and utterly satisfy
your heart...with Himself.

AMY CARMICHAEL

I will send down showers in season;

there will be showers of blessing.

EZEKIEL 34:26 NIV

APRIL 10

APRIL 11

*S*pring bursts today,
For love is risen and all the earth's at play.

CHRISTINA ROSSETTI

*N*othing great was ever done
without much enduring.

CATHERINE OF SIENA

My...sisters, whenever you face trials of any kind,
consider it nothing but joy,...and let endurance have
its full effect, so that you may be mature and
complete, lacking in nothing.

JAMES 1:2,4 NRSV

APRIL 12

APRIL 13

*T*he measure of a life, after all, is not
its duration but its donation.

CORRIE TEN BOOM

*A*s women, we want to know
we are important and that we have a
significant place in our world. We need to
know that we matter to someone, that our
lives are making a difference in the lives of
other people, that we are able to touch their
souls. This desire to have value is God-given.

BEVERLY LAHAYE

APRIL 14

APRIL 15

*T*herefore, as we have opportunity,
let us do good to all people.

GALATIANS 6:10 NIV

*I*f I can think of myself as loved, I can love and accept others. If I see myself as forgiven, I can be gracious toward others. If I see myself as powerful, I can do what I know is right. If I see myself as full, I can give myself freely to others.

KATHY PEEL

APRIL 16

APRIL 17

*N*o one can arrive from being
talented alone. God gives talent,
work transforms talent into genius.

ANNA PAVLOVA

*B*y putting the gift of yearning
for God into every human being's heart,
God at the same time draws all people
made in God's image to God's self and
into their own true selves.

ROBERTA BONDI

APRIL 18

APRIL 19

*I*f I'm not free to fail, I'm not
free to take risks, and everything in life
that's worth doing involves a willingness to
take a risk and involves the risk of failure....
I have to try, but I do not have to succeed.

MADELEINE L'ENGLE

*C*ast your cares on the Lord
and he will sustain you.

PSALM 55:22 NIV

APRIL 20

APRIL 21

*W*omen of adventure have conquered
their fates and know how to live exciting
and fulfilling lives right where they are.
They have learned to reinvent themselves
and find creative ways to enjoy the world and
their place in it. They know how to take
mini-vacations, stop and smell the roses,
and live fully in the moment.

BARBARA JENKINS

*F*ar away, there in the sunshine,
are my highest aspirations.... I can
look up and see their beauty, believe
in them, and try to follow where they lead.

LOUISA MAY ALCOTT

APRIL 22

APRIL 23

*I*n the deepest heart of
every person God planted a longing
for Himself, as He is: a God of love.

EUGENIA PRICE

*Y*our example is much more powerful
than anything you can ever say.

ELISABETH ELLIOT

APRIL 24

APRIL 25

$\mathcal{L}$ive out your God-created identity.
Live generously and graciously toward others,
the way God lives toward you.

MATTHEW 5:48 THE MESSAGE

*T*here is something very powerful about...
someone believing in you, someone giving
you another chance.

SHEILA WALSH

APRIL 26

APRIL 27

*M*ay your life become one of glad
and unending praise to the Lord as you
journey through this world, and in the
world that is to come!

TERESA OF AVILA

You've always been great toward me—what love!...
You, O God, are both tender and kind, not easily
angered, immense in love, and you never, never quit.

PSALM 86:13,15 THE MESSAGE

*H*appiness is excitement that has found a settling down place, but there is always a little corner that keeps flapping around.

E. L. KONIGSBURG

APRIL 28

APRIL 29

*Y*our outward appearance is
never as important as your heart.
That's what's eternally significant.

LORI HANSEN

$\mathcal{S}$ee! The winter is past;

the rains are over and gone.

Flowers appear on the earth;

the season of singing has come.

SONG OF SOLOMON 2:11-12 NIV

APRIL 30

MAY 1

*O*ur job is not to straighten each
other out, but to help each other up.

NEVA COYLE

$\mathcal{K}$ind words are jewels
that live in the heart and soul
and remain as blessed memories
years after they have been spoken.

MARVEA JOHNSON

MAY 2

MAY 3

*F*riendship is meeting another's
needs in a practical way.

BEVERLY LaHAYE

*G*od has designs on our future...
and He has designed us for the future.
He has given us something to do in the
future that no one else can do.

RUTH SENTER

MAY 4

MAY 5

*W*hat matters is not your
outer appearance—the styling of your hair,
the jewelry you wear, the cut of your
clothes—but your inner disposition.
Cultivate inner beauty, the gentle,
gracious kind that God delights in.

1 PETER 3:3-4 THE MESSAGE

$\mathcal{W}$e may run, walk, stumble, drive, or fly, but let us never lose sight of the reason for the journey, or miss a chance to see a rainbow on the way.

GLORIA GAITHER

MAY 6

MAY 7

*J*oy is a net of love by which
you can catch souls.

MOTHER TERESA

$\mathcal{W}$hatever job I perform—whether changing a diaper, closing a deal, teaching a class, or writing a book—when I meet legitimate needs, I am carrying on God's work.

KATHY PEEL

MAY 8

MAY 9

*O*n Mother's Day, I think moms
should be able to wake up and say to
themselves: I'm not just a housewife,
I'm a domestic goddess!

BARBARA JOHNSON

*M*ay God who gives patience,
steadiness, and encouragement help you to
live in complete harmony with each other.

ROMANS 15:5 TLB

MAY 10

MAY 11

*T*here is nothing so kingly as kindness,

And nothing so royal as truth.

ALICE CARY

*I*n a special way, human beings...being made in the image of God, only become real human beings, are only able to grow and thrive as human beings as they also yearn for God.

ROBERTA BONDI

MAY 12

MAY 13

*W*orry does not empty
tomorrow of its sorrow; it empties
today of its strength.

CORRIE TEN BOOM

*O*pinion is a flitting thing,

But Truth outlasts the Sun—

If then we cannot own them both—

Possess the oldest one.

EMILY DICKINSON

I have chosen the way of truth; I have set my heart
on your laws.... I run in the path of your commands,
for you have set my heart free.

PSALM 119:30,32 NIV

MAY 14

MAY 15

*D*on't become so well-adjusted to your culture that you fit into it without even thinking. Instead, fix your attention on God. You'll be changed from the inside out. Readily recognize what he wants from you, and quickly respond to it. Unlike the culture around you, always dragging you down to its level of immaturity, God brings the best out of you, develops well-formed maturity in you.

ROMANS 12:2 THE MESSAGE

*C*ourage...is when you know you're
licked before you begin, but you begin
anyway and you see it through no
matter what.

HARPER LEE

MAY 16

MAY 17

*I*f it can be verified, we don't need faith.... Faith is for that which lies on the other side of reason. Faith is what makes life bearable, with all its tragedies and ambiguities and sudden, startling joys.

MADELEINE L'ENGLE

*I*nfluence often isn't noticed
until it blossoms later in the garden of
someone else's life. Our words and actions
may land close to home, or they may
be carried far and wide.

PAM FARREL

MAY 18

MAY 19

$\mathcal{T}$he best and most beautiful things
in the world cannot be seen or even touched.
They must be felt with the heart.

HELEN KELLER

*S*o, chosen by God for this new
life of love, dress in the wardrobe God
picked out for you: compassion, kindness,
humility, quiet strength, discipline.

COLOSSIANS 3:12 THE MESSAGE

MAY 20

MAY 21

A friend is one who says,
I've time, when others have to rush.

JUNE MASTERS BACHER

*N*othing strengthens the judgment
and quickens the conscience like
individual responsibility.

ELIZABETH CADY STANTON

MAY 22

MAY 23

*G*od is the sunshine that warms
us, the rain that melts the frost and
waters the young plants. The presence
of God is a climate of strong and
bracing love, always there.

JOAN ARNOLD

*B*ut God has promised strength for
the day, Rest for the labor, light for the way,
Grace for the trials, help from above,
Unfailing sympathy, undying love.

ANNIE JOHNSON FLINT

MAY 24

MAY 25

A wise person gets known
for insight; gracious words add to
one's reputation.

PROVERBS 16:21 THE MESSAGE

*F*aith isn't the ability to believe
long and far into the misty future.
It's simply taking God at His word
and taking the next step.

JONI EARECKSON TADA

MAY 26

MAY 27

To live is so startling it leaves little time for anything else.

EMILY DICKINSON

*T*o be a joy-bearer and a joy-giver says everything, for in our life, if one is joyful, it means that one is faithfully living for God, and that nothing else counts; and if one gives joy to others one is doing God's work; with joy without and joy within, all is well.... I can conceive no higher way.

JANET ERSKINE STUART

MAY 28

MAY 29

$\mathcal{Y}$ou pay God a compliment by
asking great things of Him.

TERESA OF AVILA

$\mathcal{D}$ear friend, guard Clear Thinking and Common Sense with your life; don't for a minute lose sight of them. They'll keep your soul alive and well, they'll keep you fit and attractive.

PROVERBS 3:21-22 THE MESSAGE

MAY 30

MAY 31

*N*othing we can do will make the
Father love us less; nothing we do can
make Him love us more. He loves us
unconditionally with an everlasting love.
All He asks of us is that we respond to
Him with the free will that
He has given to us.

NANCIE CARMICHAEL

*W*holehearted, ready laughter heals, encourages, relaxes anyone within hearing distance. The laughter that springs from love makes wide the space around it—gives room for the loved one to enter in. Real laughter welcomes, and never shuts out.

EUGENIA PRICE

JUNE 1

JUNE 2

*W*e must know that we have been
created for greater things, not just to be a
number in the world, not just to go for
diplomas and degrees, this work and that
work. We have been created in order
to love and to be loved.

MOTHER TERESA

*A*lthough I am thankful for my career, being a good wife and mom is as important as anything else I do.

KATHY PEEL

JUNE 3

JUNE 4

"For I know the plans I have
for you," declares the Lord, "plans to
prosper you and not to harm you,
plans to give you hope and a future."

JEREMIAH 29:11 NIV

*C*onsider this—many times people
on the other side of the fence are
admiring how green your grass is!

BEVERLY LaHAYE

JUNE 5

JUNE 6

*F*riends remind us we are part
of something greater than ourselves,
a larger world, and the right friends
keep us on track.

BARBARA JENKINS

*W*e never know how high we are
Till we are called to rise;
And then, if we are true to plan,
Our statures touch the skies.

EMILY DICKINSON

Finally...whatever is true, whatever is honorable,
whatever is right, whatever is pure, whatever is
lovely, whatever is of good repute, if there is any
excellence and if anything worthy of praise, let
your mind dwell on these things.

PHILIPPIANS 4:8-9 NASB

JUNE 7

JUNE 8

*T*he best reason to pray is that God is really there. In praying, our unbelief gradually starts to melt. God moves smack into the middle of even an ordinary day....Prayer is a matter of keeping at it.... Thunderclaps and lightning flashes are very unlikely. It is well to start small and quietly.

EMILIE GRIFFIN

*N*ow glory be to God who by his mighty power at work within us is able to do far more than we would ever dare to ask or even dream of—infinitely beyond our highest prayers, desires, thoughts, or hopes.

EPHESIANS 3:20 TLB

JUNE 9

JUNE 10

*D*on't be afraid to tell God exactly how you feel (He's already read your thoughts anyway).

ELISABETH ELLIOT

$\mathcal{T}$he moments of happiness we enjoy take us by surprise. It is not that we seize them, but that they seize us.

ASHLEY MONTAGU

JUNE 11

JUNE 12

*Y*ou are God's created beauty
and the focus of His
affection and delight.

JANET L. WEAVER SMITH

$\mathcal{T}$oo often the I-can-handle-it-myself society we live in seems to promote loneliness rather than friendship. Friends are an important part of sharing the burden and worry of each day.

SHERI CURRY

JUNE 13

JUNE 14

*T*hough I am surrounded by troubles,
you will bring me safely through them....
Your power will save me. The Lord will
work out his plans for my life—for your
loving-kindness, Lord, continues forever.

PSALM 138:7-8 TLB

$\mathscr{M}$iracles are instantaneous,
they cannot be summoned, but come of
themselves, usually at unlikely moments and
to those who least expect them.

KATHERINE ANNE PORTER

JUNE 15

JUNE 16

*S*o wait before the Lord. Wait in
the stillness. And in that stillness, assurance
will come to you. You will know that you are
heard; you will know that your Lord ponders
the voice of your humble desires; you will
hear quiet words spoken to you yourself,
perhaps to your grateful surprise
and refreshment.

AMY CARMICHAEL

*O*h, the comfort—the inexpressible comfort of feeling safe with a person—having neither to weigh thoughts nor measure words, but pouring them all right out, just as they are, chaff and grain together; certain that a faithful hand will take and sift them, keep what is worth keeping, and then with the breath of kindness blow the rest away.

DINAH MARIA MULOCK CRAIK

JUNE 17

JUNE 18

o outside, to the fields, enjoy
nature and the sunshine, go out and
try to recapture happiness in yourself and
in God. Think of all the beauty that's
still left in and around you and be happy!

ANNE FRANK

*C*harm is deceptive, and beauty
is fleeting; but a woman who
fears the Lord is to be praised.

PROVERBS 31:30 NIV

JUNE 19

JUNE 20

*C*haracter cannot be developed in ease and quiet. Only through experience of trial and suffering can the soul be strengthened, vision cleared, ambition inspired, and success achieved.

HELEN KELLER

To be rooted is perhaps the most important and least recognized need of the human soul.

SIMONE WEIL

JUNE 21

JUNE 22

*T*ruth is always exciting.
Speak it, then. Life is dull without it.

PEARL S. BUCK

*P*rayer is the deliberate and
persevering action of the soul. It is true
and enduring, and full of grace.
Prayer fastens the soul to God and
makes it one with God's will.

JULIAN OF NORWICH

JUNE 23

JUNE 24

*H*e surrounds me with loving-kindness
and tender mercies. He fills my life
with good things!

PSALM 103:4-5 TLB

*T*uck [this] thought into your heart today. Treasure it. Your Father God cares about your daily everythings that concern you.

KAY ARTHUR

JUNE 25

JUNE 26

*E*very act of kindness
Moves to a larger one
Till friendships bloom to show
What little deeds have done.

JUNE MASTERS BACHER

*T*he depth of a friendship—how much
it means to us...depends, at least in part,
upon how many parts of ourselves a friend
sees, shares, and validates.

LILLIAN RUBIN

JUNE 27

JUNE 28

*H*ospitality is making your
guests feel at home even though
you wish they were.

BARBARA JOHNSON

$\mathcal{L}$ove is a fruit, in season at all times and within the reach of every hand. Anyone may gather it and no limit is set.

MOTHER TERESA

JUNE 29

JUNE 30

*S*teep yourself in God-reality,
God-initiative, God-provisions. You'll find
all your everyday human concerns will be
met. Don't be afraid of missing out.
You're my dearest friends! The Father
wants to give you the very kingdom itself.

LUKE 12:31-32 THE MESSAGE

*I*f it is God who gives prayer,
then God often gives it in the form
of gratitude, and gratitude itself, when it
is received attentively in prayer, is healing
to the heart. Prayer is such a mysterious
business for something so ordinary
and everyday.

ROBERTA BONDI

JULY 1

JULY 2

A life without contemplation quickly loses depth. It becomes like a field that is all top-soil—one strong wind and it is all blown away. It is of no long-term use to anyone. Thought, reflection, engaging of the mind—these are all what it takes if we are to have something to say...if our ideas are to be clear, concise, and well developed.

RUTH SENTER

$\mathcal{S}$o where do you go when you
can't fix your life? The only place to go
is back to the One who made you.

Sheila Walsh

JULY 3

JULY 4

I am beginning to learn that
it is the sweet, simple things of life
which are the real ones after all.

LAURA INGALLS WILDER

*P*leasant words are a honeycomb,
sweet to the soul and healing to the bones.

PROVERBS 16:24 NIV

JULY 5

JULY 6

*F*eeling grateful or appreciative
of someone or something in your life
actually attracts more of the things that
you appreciate and value into your life.
And, the more of your life that you like
and appreciate, the healthier you'll be.
Science is now documenting what women
have known intuitively for millennia:
that "thinking with your heart" will lead
you in the right direction.

CHRISTIANE NORTHRUP

*T*he way may at times
seem dark, but light will arise
if you trust in the Lord and
wait patiently for Him.

ELIZABETH T. KING

JULY 7

JULY 8

*I*f you believe in a God who controls the big things, you have to believe in a God who controls the little things. It is we, of course, to whom things look "little" or "big."

ELISABETH ELLIOT

*T*rue worth is in being, not seeming—
In doing, each day that goes by,
Some little good—not in dreaming
Of great things to do by and by.

ALICE CARY

JULY 9

JULY 10

The Lord is good, a refuge in times of trouble. He cares for those who trust in him.

NAHUM 1:7 NIV

$\mathcal{S}$uccess is often possible
only with intense action accompanied
by persistent will. Persistence is
taking one more step.

PAM FARREL

JULY 11

JULY 12

The beauty of a woman is
not in the clothes she wears,
The figure that she carries, or the way
she combs her hair.
The beauty of a woman must
be seen from in her eyes,
Because that is the doorway to her heart,
the place where love resides.

AUDREY HEPBURN

*I*t is an extraordinary and beautiful thing that God, in creation...works with the beauty of matter; the reality of things; the discoveries of the senses, all five of them; so that we, in turn, may hear the grass growing; see a face springing to life in love and laughter.... The offerings of creation...our glimpses of truth.

MADELEINE L'ENGLE

JULY 13

JULY 14

*B*e dependable...to yourself as well as others. Know that others can depend on you to do what you promise to or need to. And depend on yourself to do something that pleases you each and every day.

KATHY PEEL

*B*e of one mind, live in peace;
and the God of love and peace
shall be with you.

2 CORINTHIANS 13:11 KJV

JULY 15

JULY 16

*H*appy people...enjoy the fundamental, often very simple things of life.... They savor the moment, glad to be alive, enjoying their work, their families, the good things around them. They are adaptable; they can bend with the wind, adjust to the changes in their times, enjoy the contest of life.... Their eyes are turned outward; they are aware, compassionate. They have the capacity to love.

JANE CANFIELD

*I*f you surrender completely
to the moments as they pass,
you live more richly those moments.

ANNE MORROW LINDBERGH

JULY 17

JULY 18

*E*veryone has a gift for something,
even if it is the gift of being a good friend.

Marian Anderson

God has given each of you some special abilities;
be sure to use them to help each other, passing on
to others God's many kinds of blessings.

1 Peter 4:10 TLB

*U*nhappiness does not necessarily come from not having this or that. If we have each other, we have everything.

MOTHER TERESA

JULY 19

JULY 20

*Y*ou're blessed when you care.
At the moment of being "care-full,"
you find yourselves cared for. You're blessed
when you get your inside world—your mind
and heart—put right. Then you can see
God in the outside world.

MATTHEW 5:7-8 THE MESSAGE

*I*n the end, those things that affect your life most deeply are too simple to talk about.

NELL BLAINE

JULY 21

JULY 22

*W*e don't need soft skies to make
friendship a joy to us. What a heavenly thing
it is; World without end, truly. I grow warm
thinking of it, and should glow at the
thought.... Such friends God has given
me in this little life of mine!

CELIA LAIGHTON THAXTER

I am convinced beyond a shadow
of any doubt that the most valuable pursuit
we can embark upon is to know God.

KAY ARTHUR

JULY 23

JULY 24

*L*ord...teach me to live this
moment only, looking neither to the
past with regret, nor to the future
with apprehension. Let love be
my aim and my life a prayer.

ROSEANN ALEXANDER-ISHAM

*H*ow precious it is, Lord, to realize
that you are thinking about me constantly!
I can't even count how many times a day
your thoughts turn towards me.

PSALM 139:17-18 TLB

JULY 25

JULY 26

*T*he well of Providence
is deep. It's the buckets we bring
to it that are small.

MARY WEBB

*W*hat the dew is to the flower,
Gentle words are to the soul.

POLLY RUPE

JULY 27

JULY 28

*F*aithful friends, like diamonds,
withstand the test of time.

BEVERLY LaHAYE

*T*he things that matter the most
in this world, they can never be
held in our hand.

GLORIA GAITHER

JULY 29

JULY 30

*T*he Lord will guide you always;
he will satisfy your needs in a sun-scorched
land.... You will be like a well-watered
garden, like a spring whose waters never fail.

ISAIAH 58:11 NIV

*I*t is always wise to stop wishing
for things long enough to enjoy the
fragrance of those now flowering.

PATRICE GIFFORD

JULY 31

AUGUST 1

*T*o act lovingly is to begin to feel loving,
and certainly to act joyfully brings joy to
others, which in turn makes one feel joyful.
I believe we are called to the duty of delight.

DOROTHY DAY

*A*s a rose fills a room
with its fragrance, so will God's
love fill our lives.

MARGARET BROWNLEY

AUGUST 2

AUGUST 3

*Y*ou can't turn back the clock.
But you can wind it up again.

BONNIE PRUDEN

$\mathcal{H}$e who refreshes others
will himself be refreshed.

PROVERBS 11:25 NIV

AUGUST 4

AUGUST 5

*T*ime is a very precious gift of God;
so precious that it's only given to
us moment by moment.

AMELIA BARR

*M*any persons have a wrong
idea of what constitutes real happiness.
It is not obtained through self-gratification,
but through fidelity to a worthy purpose.

HELEN KELLER

AUGUST 6

AUGUST 7

*L*et none glory in her success
but refer all to God in deepest
thankfulness; on the other hand, no failure
should dishearten her as long as she
has done her best.

MOTHER TERESA

*L*ive your life while you have it.
Life is a splendid gift—there is
nothing small about it.

FLORENCE NIGHTINGALE

AUGUST 8

AUGUST 9

*F*or God is sheer beauty,

all-generous in love,

loyal always and ever.

PSALM 100:5 THE MESSAGE

*J*oy is elusive.... It flows most freely when we stop trying to make it happen. We do not come to joy. Joy comes to us.

RUTH SENTER

AUGUST 10

AUGUST 11

*T*rust your friends with both
the delightful and the difficult
parts of your life.

LUCI SHAW

*R*emember that one thing we all
have in common is twenty-four hours a day.
It is up to me how I choose to spend it.

KATHY PEEL

AUGUST 12

AUGUST 13

*H*aving it all doesn't necessarily
mean having it all at once.

STEPHANIE LUETKEHAUS

*N*o test or temptation that comes your way is beyond the course of what others have had to face. All you need to remember is that God will never let you down; he'll never let you be pushed past your limit; he'll always be there to help you come through it.

1 CORINTHIANS 10:13 THE MESSAGE

AUGUST 14

AUGUST 15

*I*t is my calling to treat every
human being with grace and dignity,
to treat every person, whether encountered
in a palace or a gas station, as a life
made in the image of God.

SHEILA WALSH

Oh, better than the minting

Of a gold-crowned king

Is the safe-kept memory

Of a lovely thing.

SARA TEASDALE

AUGUST 16

AUGUST 17

*S*ome people, no matter how old
they get, never lose their beauty.
They merely move it from
their faces to their hearts.

BARBARA JOHNSON

$\mathcal{L}$ove comes when we take
the time to understand and
care for another person.

Janette Oke

AUGUST 18

AUGUST 19

*O*ur God gives you everything
you need, makes you everything
you're to be.

2 THESSALONIANS 1:2 THE MESSAGE

*I*magination is the highest

kite one can fly.

Lauren Bacall

August 20

AUGUST 21

*S*omething deep in all of us
yearns for God's beauty, and we can
find it no matter where we are.

SUE MONK KIDD

*I*t is always possible to be thankful
for what is given rather than to
complain about what is not given.
One or the other becomes a habit of life.

ELISABETH ELLIOT

AUGUST 22

AUGUST 23

A friend is someone who
understands your past, believes in your
future, and accepts you today
just the way you are.

BEVERLY LaHAYE

*I*sn't everything you have and everything you are sheer gifts from God?... You already have all you need.

1 CORINTHIANS 4:7-8 THE MESSAGE

AUGUST 24

AUGUST 25

*W*hat a circus we women
perform every day of our lives.
It puts a trapeze artist to shame.

ANNE MORROW LINDBERGH

*L*ife is what happens to you
when you're making other plans.

BETTY TALMADGE

AUGUST 26

AUGUST 27

*T*hat it will never come again is
what makes life so sweet.

EMILY DICKINSON

Pursue a righteous life—a life of wonder, faith, love,
steadiness, courtesy. Run hard and fast in the faith.
Seize the eternal life, the life you were called to.

1 TIMOTHY 6:11-12 THE MESSAGE

$\mathcal{G}$od looks at the world through
the eyes of love. If we, therefore, as human
beings made in the image of God also want
to see reality rationally, that is, as it truly is,
then we, too, must learn to look at
what we see with love.

ROBERTA BONDI

AUGUST 28

AUGUST 29

*T*he right word at the right
time is like a custom-made piece of jewelry,
And a wise friend's timely reprimand is
like a gold ring slipped on your finger.

PROVERBS 25:11-12 THE MESSAGE

*W*e are so preciously loved
by God that we cannot even
comprehend it. No created being
can ever know how much and
how sweetly and tenderly
God loves them.

JULIAN OF NORWICH

AUGUST 30

AUGUST 31

*W*hen the sun shines
on you, you see your friends.
Friends are the thermometers
by which one may judge the
temperature of our fortunes.

COUNTESS OF BLESSINGTON

*O*ptimism is the faith that leads to achievement. Nothing can be done without hope.

HELEN KELLER

SEPTEMBER 1

SEPTEMBER 2

*B*ut every road is rough to me
that has no friend to cheer it.

ELIZABETH SHANE

*W*hat happens when we live God's way?
He brings gifts into our lives, much the same
way that fruit appears in an orchard—things
like affection for others, exuberance about
life, serenity. We develop a willingness to
stick with things, a sense of compassion in
the heart, and a conviction that a basic
holiness permeates things and people.

GALATIANS 5:22 THE MESSAGE

SEPTEMBER 3

SEPTEMBER 4

*T*o have a friend is to have one
of the sweetest gifts that life can bring;
to be a friend is to have a solemn and tender
education of the soul from day to day.

AMY ROBERTSON BROWN

$\mathscr{G}$od gave me a mind, and I am sure

He meant for me to use it.

KATHY PEEL

SEPTEMBER 5

SEPTEMBER 6

*I*f you think well of others,
you will also speak well of others
and to others. From the abundance of
the heart the mouth speaks. If your heart
is full of love, you will speak of love.

MOTHER TERESA

$\mathscr{T}$he way you keep your house,
the way you organize your time, the care
you take in your personal appearance,
the things you spend your money on all
speak loudly about what you believe.

ELISABETH ELLIOT

SEPTEMBER 7

SEPTEMBER 8

*N*o eye has seen, nor ear heard,

nor the human heart conceived,

what God has prepared for those who love

him.

1 CORINTHIANS 2:9 NRSV

*I*ndividuals can change things....
If everyone will just do their little part,
then we can make a tremendous difference
in the lives of other people.

SARAH PURCELL

SEPTEMBER 9

SEPTEMBER 10

*O*ur lives are a mosaic of little things,
like putting a rose in a vase on the table.

INGRID TROBISCH

$\mathcal{Y}$ou grow up the day you have
your first real laugh—at yourself.

ETHEL BARRYMORE

SEPTEMBER 11

SEPTEMBER 12

*W*e should look for reasons
to celebrate—a raise, a promotion, an
A on a paper—even a good hair day.

PAM FARREL

*T*he Lord is my strength and my shield;
my heart trusts in him and I am helped.

PSALM 28:7 NIV

SEPTEMBER 13

SEPTEMBER 14

*I*t doesn't take monumental feats
to make the world a better place.
It can be as simple as letting someone go
ahead of you in a grocery line.

BARBARA JOHNSON

*B*lessed are those who can give without remembering, and take without forgetting.

\Elizabeth Bibesco

SEPTEMBER 15

SEPTEMBER 16

*A*s women, we want to be in
harmony with our surroundings and
to contribute to our society in
meaningful and valued ways.

BEVERLY LAHAYE

$\mathcal{T}$he first requirement for growth
in self understanding is an unswerving
commitment to honesty with one's self.
No one can break our chains for us,
we have to do this for ourselves.

ELIZABETH O'CONNOR

SEPTEMBER 17

SEPTEMBER 18

To enjoy your work and to accept your lot in life—that is indeed a gift from God. The person who does that will not need to look back with sorrow on his past, for God gives him joy.

ECCLESIASTES 5:20 TLB

$\mathcal{T}$ime is a dressmaker
specializing in alterations.

FAITH BALDWIN

SEPTEMBER 19

SEPTEMBER 20

*I*t is not my business to think
about myself. My business is to think
about God. It is for God
to think about me.

SIMONE WEIL

There is no surprise more
magical than the surprise of being
loved. It is the finger of God on
a person's shoulder.

MARGARET KENNEDY

SEPTEMBER 21

SEPTEMBER 22

*T*he beauty of a woman is not in a facial mole,

But true beauty in a woman is reflected in her soul.

It is the caring that she lovingly gives,

the passion that she shows,

And the beauty of a woman with

passing years—only grows!

AUDREY HEPBURN

$\mathcal{W}$ithout God, it is utterly
impossible. But with God
everything is possible.

MARK 10:27 TLB

SEPTEMBER 23

SEPTEMBER 24

*C*herish your human connections:
your relationships with friends and family.

BARBARA BUSH

One thing I realized about having
a girlfriend is that I can't tell you who I am
without telling you who my girlfriend is.
Our relationships with other women are part
of the ground of our being. So I can't say
who I am without talking about my female
friend and who she is in my life. We discover
ourselves through our girlfriends; it's a
mutual process of self-discovery.

SUE MONK KIDD

SEPTEMBER 25

SEPTEMBER 26

*T*here are times when encouragement
means such a lot. And a word is enough
to convey it.

GRACE STRICKER DAWSON

There is something basic about friendship. It is like the structure that holds up a building. It is mostly hidden and absolutely essential.

EMILIE BARNES

SEPTEMBER 27

SEPTEMBER 28

A cheerful heart is good medicine.

PROVERBS 17:22 NIV

$\mathcal{L}$ife begets life.
Energy creates energy.
It is by spending oneself
that one becomes rich.

SARAH BERNHARDT

SEPTEMBER 29

SEPTEMBER 30

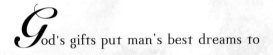

*G*od's gifts put man's best dreams to
shame.
ELIZABETH BARRETT BROWNING

Let us not get tired of doing what is right, for after
a while we will reap a harvest of blessing.

GALATIANS 6:9 TLB

*F*or memory has painted this perfect day,
with colors that never fade.
And we find at the end of a perfect day,
the soul of a friend we've made.

CARRIE JACOBS BOND

OCTOBER 1

OCTOBER 2

I believe that we are always
attracted to what we need most, an instinct
leading us toward the persons who are to
open new vistas in our lives and fill them
with new knowledge.

HELENE ISWOLSKI

*T*he moral climate of our world
depends greatly on the stature of its women.

BEVERLY LaHAYE

OCTOBER 3

OCTOBER 4

*W*hat you say goes, God, and stays,
as permanent as the heavens. Your truth
never goes out of fashion; it's up-to-date as
the earth when the sun comes up. Your
Word and truth are dependable as ever.

PSALM 119:89-91 THE MESSAGE

$\mathcal{I}$ntegrity pays. Integrity opens
doors because people learn to trust you.

PAM FARREL

OCTOBER 5

OCTOBER 6

*M*ost new discoveries are
suddenly-seen things that were always there.

SUSANNE K. LANGER

*T*he day is done, the sun has set,

Yet light still tints the sky;

My heart stands still

In reverence,

For God is passing by.

RUTH ALLA WAGER

OCTOBER 7

OCTOBER 8

*I*t isn't the great big pleasures
that count the most; it's making a great
deal out of the little ones.

JEAN WEBSTER

*D*o you want to stand out?
Then step down. Be a servant. If you puff
yourself up, you'll get the wind knocked out
of you. But if you're content to simply be
yourself, your life will count for plenty.

MATTHEW 23:11-12 THE MESSAGE

OCTOBER 9

OCTOBER 10

*S*ome people regard discipline
as a chore. For me, it is a kind of order
that sets me free to fly.

JULIE ANDREWS

A good friendship allows for diversity.
Think how boring it would be if we
all agreed with each other!

LUCI SHAW

OCTOBER 11

OCTOBER 12

*A*fter trying so hard to conform
to the standards and tastes of others,
I began to see I am a one-of-a-kind
work of art, unlike anyone else
who has ever lived or ever will.

KATHY PEEL

I know that God is faithful.
I know that He answers prayers, many
times in ways I may not understand.

SHEILA WALSH

OCTOBER 13

OCTOBER 14

*Y*ou will keep in perfect peace
him whose mind is steadfast,
because he trusts in you.

ISAIAH 26:3 NIV

*G*od, with all His giving heart,
can only give us Himself as we recognize
the depth of the need in our own lives.

EUGENIA PRICE

OCTOBER 15

OCTOBER 16

One cannot collect all the
beautiful shells on the beach.
One can collect only a few, and
they are more beautiful if they are few.

ANNE MORROW LINDBERGH

*P*rayer unites the soul to God,
for although the soul may always be like
God in nature and substance, it is often
unlike Him in condition.

JULIAN OF NORWICH

OCTOBER 17

OCTOBER 18

So shall a friendship fill each heart

With perfume sweet as roses are,

That even though we be apart,

We'll scent the fragrance from afar.

GEORGIA MCCOY

*I*f you don't know what you're
doing, pray to the Father. He loves to help.
You'll get his help, and won't be
condescended to when you ask for it.
Ask boldly, believing, without
a second thought.

JAMES 1:5-6 THE MESSAGE

OCTOBER 19

OCTOBER 20

*M*ake the least of all that
goes and the most of all that comes.
Don't regret what is past. Cherish what
you have. Look forward to all that is to
come. And most important of all, rely
moment by moment on Jesus.

GIGI GRAHAM TCHIVIDJIAN

A friend is a person with whom you dare to be yourself.

PAM BROWN

OCTOBER 21

OCTOBER 22

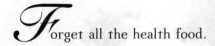

*F*orget all the health food.
We need all the preservatives we can get.

BARBARA JOHNSON

$\mathscr{N}$ever be afraid to trust an unknown future to an all-knowing God.

CORRIE TEN BOOM

OCTOBER 23

OCTOBER 24

*N*ow you're dressed in a new
wardrobe. Every item of your new way of life
is custom-made by the Creator, with his label
on it. All the old fashions are now obsolete....
From now on everyone is defined by Christ,
everyone is included in Christ.

COLOSSIANS 3:10-11 THE MESSAGE

*L*et's concentrate on a
worthwhile goal: that no child be unwanted,
that no person go unloved. And let's not
stop smiling at whomever we meet,
especially when it's hard to smile.

MOTHER TERESA

OCTOBER 25

OCTOBER 26

*W*e are of such value to God that
He came to live among us...and to guide us
home. He will go to any length to seek us,
even to being lifted high upon the cross to
draw us back to Himself. We can only
respond by loving God for His love.

CATHERINE OF SIENA

*A*n archaeologist is the best husband
any woman can have: the older she gets,
the more interested he is in her.

AGATHA CHRISTIE

OCTOBER 27

OCTOBER 28

*F*ace your deficiencies and acknowledge
them; but do not let them master you.
Let them teach you patience, sweetness,
insight. When we do the best we can, we
never know what miracle is wrought in
our life, or in the life of another.

HELEN KELLER

*Y*ou have made known to me
the path of life; you will fill me with
joy in your presence, with eternal
pleasures at your right hand.

PSALM 16:11 NIV

OCTOBER 29

OCTOBER 30

*H*appiness comes of the
capacity to feel deeply, to enjoy simply,
to think freely, to risk life, to be needed.

STORM JAMESON

*H*old fast your dreams!
Within your heart
Keep one still, secret spot
Where dreams may go
And, sheltered so,
May thrive and grow
Where doubt and fear are not.
O keep a place apart,
Within your heart,
For little dreams to go!

LOUISE DRISCOLL

OCTOBER 31

NOVEMEBR 1

$\mathcal{T}$reat your friends as you do your
pictures, and place them in their best light.

JENNIE JEROME CHURCHILL

*T*ime has a way of defining true friends.
I have discovered that passing years and
growing distance are ineffective obstacles to
the mutual love between my friends and me.

EMILIE BARNES

NOVEMBER 2

NOVEMBER 3

*M*ay the Lord continually
bless you with heaven's blessings as
well as with human joys.

PSALM 128:5 TLB

*T*he one thing that doesn't abide
by majority rule is a person's conscience.

HARPER LEE

NOVEMBER 4

NOVEMBER 5

*I*t is the simple things of
life that make living worthwhile,
the sweet fundamental things such
as love and duty, work and rest,
and living close to nature.

LAURA INGALLS WILDER

A good laugh is as good
as a prayer sometimes.

LUCY MAUD MONTGOMERY

She is clothed with strength and dignity;

she can laugh at the days to come.

PROVERBS 31:25 NIV

NOVEMBER 6

NOVEMBER 7

*H*eroic women know their purpose
in life is not to satisfy their own desires,
but to minister healing, love, and hope
to the less fortunate.

BEVERLY LaHAYE

*A*biding love surrounds those
who trust in the Lord.

PSALM 32:10 TLB

NOVEMBER 8

November 9

If we had no winter, the spring would not be so pleasant: if we did not sometimes taste of adversity, prosperity would not be so welcome.

ANNE BRADSTREET

*O*ne can never pay in gratitude;

one can only pay "in kind"

somewhere else in life.

ANNE MORROW LINDBERGH

NOVEMBER 10

NOVEMBER 11

*P*eace is when time doesn't
matter as it passes by.

MARIA SCHNELL

*H*ospitality is not entertaining.
Hospitality is an attitude of opening up
your life so that others can come in.

PAM FARREL

NOVEMBER 12

NOVEMBER 13

Don't lose a minute in building on what you've been given, complementing your basic faith with good character, spiritual understanding, alert discipline, passionate patience, reverent wonder, warm friendliness, and generous love, each dimension fitting into and developing the others.

2 PETER 1:5 THE MESSAGE

*B*oth within the family and
without, our sisters hold up our mirrors,
our images of who we are and of who
we can dare to become.

ELIZABETH FISHEL

NOVEMBER 14

NOVEMBER 15

*I*n the end, I think this is
what women truly desire: to know God
and to stand tall in their faith, strong
at the core, tender in heart.

RUTH SENTER

A friend understands what
you are trying to say...even when your
thoughts aren't fitting into words.

ANN D. PARRISH

NOVEMBER 16

NOVEMBER 17

*N*ever eat more than you can lift.

MISS PIGGY

_**M**ay you be given more and
more of God's kindness, peace, and love._

JUDE 1:2 TLB

NOVEMBER 18

November 19

*W*hen we call on God, He bends down
His ear to listen, as a father bends down
to listen to his little child.

ELIZABETH CHARLES

*W*e should realize that
poverty doesn't only consist in being
hungry for bread, but rather it is a
tremendous hunger for human dignity.
We need to love and to be somebody
for someone else.

MOTHER TERESA

NOVEMBER 20

NOVEMBER 21

*O*ne of the most joyful discoveries
of life is that in recognizing, affirming,
and comforting another person we find
ourselves recognized, affirmed, and comforted.

ELISABETH ELLIOT

*T*here is always a lot to be thankful for if you take the time to look for it. Right now, I am sitting here thinking how nice it is that wrinkles don't hurt.

BARBARA JOHNSON

NOVEMBER 22

NOVEMBER 23

*I*n everything you do, put God first,
and he will direct you and crown your
efforts with success.

PROVERBS 3:6 TLB

$\mathcal{T}$here is something in every season,
in every day, to celebrate with thanksgiving.

GLORIA GAITHER

NOVEMBER 24

NOVEMBER 25

$\mathcal{W}$ere there no God we would
be in this glorious world with grateful
hearts and no one to thank.

CHRISTINA ROSSETTI

$\mathcal{G}$ratitude unlocks the fullness of life.
It turns what we have into enough, and
more. It turns denial into acceptance, chaos
to order, confusion to clarity. It can turn a
meal into a feast, a house into a home, a
stranger into a friend. Gratitude makes
sense of our past, brings peace for today,
and creates a vision for tomorrow.

MELODY BEATTIE

NOVEMBER 26

NOVEMBER 27

A keen sense of humor
helps us to overlook the unbecoming,
understand the unconventional, tolerate
the unpleasant, overcome the unexpected,
and outlast the unbearable.

BILLY GRAHAM

$\mathcal{G}$ive away your life; you'll find life given back, but not merely given back—given back with bonus and blessing. Giving, not getting, is the way. Generosity begets generosity.

LUKE 6:38 THE MESSAGE

NOVEMBER 28

NOVEMBER 29

*T*he growth of understanding
follows an ascending spiral rather
than a straight line.

JOANNA FIELD

*W*elcome home! That's what I want my life to say to everyone whose path crosses mine. I want to create an atmosphere of serenity and joy, blessing and belonging, that embraces people and draws them in—that makes them feel loved and special and cared for.

EMILIE BARNES

NOVEMBER 30

DECEMBER 1

*T*have learned that to
have a good friend is the purest
of all God's gifts, for it is a love
that has no exchange of payment.

FRANCES FARMER

*W*e turn not older with years,
but newer every day.

EMILY DICKINSON

DECEMBER 2

DECEMBER 3

*T*he Lord gives strength to his people;
the Lord blesses his people with peace.

PSALM 29:11 NIV

*I*t is not how many years we live,

but what we do with them.

EVANGELINE BOOTH

DECEMBER 4

DECEMBER 5

*I*t's your love your friends
need—not expensive gifts or
extravagant surprises.

MARION GARRETTY

*T*he miracle of joy is this:
It happens when there is no apparent
reason for it. Circumstances may call for
despair. Yet something different rouses
itself inside us....We remember God.
We remember He is love.
We remember He is near.

RUTH SENTER

DECEMBER 6

DECEMBER 7

*W*hatever our situation in
life...we can and should surround
ourselves with friends who not only
understand us, but also inspire us to
make the most of our current calling.

BEVERLY LAHAYE

*W*hat a wonderful God we have—he is
the Father of our Lord Jesus Christ, the
source of every mercy, and the one who so
wonderfully comforts and strengthens us in
our hardships and trials.

2 CORINTHIANS 1:3-4 TLB

DECEMBER 8

DECEMBER 9

*I*n our family an experience was
not finished, not truly experienced, unless
written down or shared with another.

ANNE MORROW LINDBERGH

*T*o love God, to serve Him because we love Him, is...our highest happiness. Love makes all labor light. We serve with enthusiasm where we love with sincerity.

HANNAH MORE

DECEMBER 10

DECEMBER 11

*T*he greatest gift we can
give to one another is rapt attention
to one another's existence.

SUE ATCHLEY EBAUGH

*O*riginality is not doing something
no one else has ever done, but doing what
has been done countless times with
new life, new breath.

MARIE CHAPIAN

DECEMBER 12

DECEMBER 13

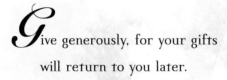

*G*ive generously, for your gifts
will return to you later.

ECCLESIASTES 11:1 TLB

$\mathcal{L}$ove comes out of heaven
unasked and unsought.

PEARL S. BUCK

DECEMBER 14

DECEMBER 15

*B*efore anything else, above all else,
beyond everything else, God loves us.
God loves us extravagantly, ridiculously,
without limit or condition. God is in love
with us...God yearns for us.

ROBERTA BONDI

$\mathcal{R}$emember, the Christmas presents
of today are the garage sales of tomorrow.

BARBARA JOHNSON

DECEMBER 16

DECEMBER 17

*F*or attractive lips,
Speak words of kindness.
For lovely eyes,
Seek out the good in people.
For a slim figure,
Share your food with the hungry.
For beautiful hair,
Let a child run his or her
fingers through it once a day.
For poise,
Walk with the knowledge you'll never walk alone.

AUDREY HEPBURN

*T*hanks be to God for
his indescribable gift!

2 CORINTHIANS 9:15 NIV

DECEMBER 18

DECEMBER 19

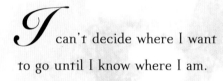

I can't decide where I want
to go until I know where I am.

ANNIE CHAPMAN

God must have said, "I know what I'll do, I'll send my LOVE right down there where they are. And I'll send it as a tiny baby, so they'll have to touch it, and they'll have to hold it close."

GLORIA GAITHER

DECEMBER 20

DECEMBER 21

*C*hristmas, my child, is love in action....
When you love someone, you give to them, as
God gives to us. The greatest gift He ever
gave was the person of His Son, sent to us in
human form so that we might know what
God the Father is really like! Every time we
love, every time we give, it's Christmas.

DALE EVANS ROGERS

*T*he coming of Jesus at Bethlehem
brought joy to the world and to every
human heart. May His coming this
Christmas bring to each one of us that
peace and joy that He desires to give.

MOTHER TERESA

DECEMBER 22

DECEMBER 23

"*T*he virgin will be with child and will give birth to a son, and they will call him Immanuel—which means, "God with us."

MATTHEW 1:23 NIV

*W*hat can I give Him

Poor as I am?

If I were a shepherd,

I would give Him a lamb,

If I were a Wise Man,

I would do my part,—

But what I can I give Him,

Give my heart.

CHRISTINA ROSSETTI

DECEMBER 24

DECEMBER 25

*I*f everything special and warm and happy in my formative years could have been consolidated into one word, that word would have been Christmas.

GLORIA GAITHER

$\mathcal{G}$od has put into each of our lives
a void that cannot be filled by the world.
We may leave God or put Him on hold,
but He is always there, patiently waiting
for us...to turn back to Him.

EMILIE BARNES

DECEMBER 26

DECEMBER 27

*J*oy is always a promise.

MADELEINE L'ENGLE

The joy of the Lord is your strength.

NEHEMIAH 8:10 TLB

*R*ecall it as often as you wish,
a happy memory never wears out.

LIBBIE FUDIM

DECEMBER 28

DECEMBER 29

*F*inally...whatever is true, whatever
is honorable, whatever is right, whatever
is pure, whatever is lovely, whatever is of
good repute, if there is any excellence and
if anything worthy of praise, let your
mind dwell on these things.

PHILIPPIANS 4:8-9 NRSV

I said to a man who stood at the gate
of the year, "Give me a light that I may tread
safely into the unknown." And he replied,
"Go out into the darkness and put your hand
in the hand of God. That shall be to you better than a light and safer than a known way."

M. LOUISE HASKINS

DECEMBER 30

DECEMBER 31

*L*ife begins each morning....
Each morning is the open door to a new
world—new vistas, new aims, new tryings.

LEIGH HODGES